World at Work
BANKING

Lynne Rushton
and Tony Hopwood

Longman

1 Why have a bank account?

STUDENTS!
What are you going to do with your grant?*

THIS?

OR THIS?

These are some of the advantages of having a bank account

- **SECURITY** — No need to carry or keep at home large amounts of cash.   UNIT 4

- **CONVENIENCE** — With a current account you can pay by cheque in restaurants, shops and petrol stations. No embarrassing shortages of cash.   3, 5, 6

- **INVESTMENT** — In a deposit account your money works for you and earns interest — at the moment 11% a year. A much better way of saving than under the mattress!   9

- **LOANS** — Want to buy something special? Not enough money? The bank may be able to lend you some.   8

- **ADVICE** — Do you have difficulty organising your finances? The bank is there to help and advise.

- **TRAVEL FACILITIES** — Going abroad? The bank can arrange travellers cheques and foreign currency. Shops and banks in many European countries now accept your normal cheques as Eurocheques.   11, 12, 13

- **ARRANGING THE FUTURE** — When the time comes, the bank can help you with all the big money problems like buying a house or running a business.   8, 10

INTERESTED? POP IN AND SEE US. IT COULD CHANGE YOUR WAY OF LIFE!

*In England university students often receive a certain amount of money from the Government to pay for their living expenses. This is called a GRANT.

Comprehension Choose the best answer.

1 With a Eurocheque account you can (a) earn 11% interest a year (b) borrow money from the bank (c) start a business (d) get cash from banks in other European countries.
2 What are the two advantages from this list of having a bank account? (a) it is safer than keeping money at home (b) the bank will give you cheques from banks in other countries (c) you don't have to organise your finances (d) you may be able to borrow money from the bank.

Hidden word puzzle

Fill in the answers to find the missing word.

HIDDEN WORD

Clues
1 Ready money
2 Safety
3 If you have money problems, the bank will talk to you and give you ____
4 Money which the bank lends you
5 Sum
6 Positive point
7 When there is a ____ of something it means you haven't got enough

1 C
2 S
3 A
4 L
5 A
6 A
7 S

Where to find information in this book

The following people need banking services. Next to each person, write down the numbers of the units in this book which would give them the information they need.

1 Peter Barker, a young computer programmer, wants to buy a car, but doesn't have enough money. Unit ......
2 Nigel Major, a businessman, travels around the country and needs to pay a lot of people. Units ......
3 Susan Calvin, a doctor, is going on holiday to Greece this summer. Units ......
4 David Wheeler and Jane Pettigrew are going to get married next month. Units ......
5 Daniel Johns has just left college and wants to start a garage business. Units ......
6 Rosie Plant has just inherited £2,000 from her aunt. Unit ......

Helping a friend

One of your friends is thinking of opening a bank account. Can you answer his questions?

1 If all my money is in a bank, how can I pay in shops and restaurants?
   ....
2 How can a bank account help me to earn money?
   ....
3 How can a bank help if I want to go abroad?
   ....
4 How can a bank help me to arrange my future?
   ....

2 Opening an account

> **DO YOU KNOW? 1**
> When you open a bank account you must give the names and addresses of 2 people to the bank. These people are asked to write a short letter, called a reference, about your character.

> **DO YOU KNOW? 2**
> In England you can open a bank account with as little as £1. Two people can open an account together. This is called a joint account.

Putting money into your account When you open an account you have to put some money into it. Every time you put money into the bank you use a paying-in slip.

CUSTOMER: I'd like to pay my salary cheque and some cash into my account.

CLERK: Well, *you fill in* the amount of the cheque here ①.
With the cash, *write* the amount of notes and coins at the side ② then *put* the total here ③. You have three £10 notes, two £1 notes and 36p, so you write it like this. Then *you should add up* the total amount and put it here ④.

Date 26/10/1982		
Notes: £20		
£10	30	—
£5		
£1	2	—
Coins: 50p		
Silver		35
Bronze		1
Total of cash	32	36
Cheques etc.	348	21
Cashier's stamp and initials ⑦ £	380	57

SHOESTRING BANK LIMITED
Current account credit

Date ⑤ 26/10/1982
Cashier's stamp and initials

COMPLETE IN BLOCK LETTERS PLEASE

| Account holding branch HIGH ST, MORGANTOWN |
| Account in name of MELANIE ATKINS |
| Account Number 0 6 4 3 4 9 8 |
| Paid in by ⑥ M. J. Atkins |

Notes: £20		②
£10	30	—
£5		
£1	2	—
Coins: 50p		
Silver		35
Bronze		1
Total of cash ③	32	36
Total of Cheques ①	348	21
£ ④	380	57

CUSTOMER: What's the 'account holding branch'?

CLERK: That's the branch where you have your account. Underneath you *should put* the name which is printed on your cheques and the account number. Then, *could you put* the date here ⑤ and your signature at the bottom? ⑥

CUSTOMER: What's this for? ⑦

CLERK: That's your counterfoil. *If you fill in* the details of your deposit here, you can keep it as a record for yourself.

CUSTOMER: Thanks very much for your help.

> **DO YOU KNOW? 3**
> The bank asks for an example of your signature, called a specimen signature.

> **DO YOU KNOW? 4**
> You pay the bank a commission or account charge for their services. In some banks, if you keep a certain amount of credit in your account, these services are free of charge.

True or false? Look at the statements below and tick (√) if you think they are true or false. Can you correct the false statements?

	TRUE	FALSE
1 You do not have to put any money into your account when you first open it.		
2 The bank charges a commission for its services.		
3 It is not possible to share an account with someone.		
4 You need two references to open a bank account.		

Hidden word puzzle

Fill in the puzzle and find the missing word. Use these clues to help you.

Clues
1 The money you earn
2 ____ of charge means you do not have to pay
3 The section of a form where you put the details for your own record
4 To ____ an account (start)
5 The office of a bank, in your town
6 A ____ signature is an example for the bank
7 Metal pieces of money
8 Someone who works in a bank
9 Paper money

HIDDEN WORD

1 S
2 F
3 C
4 O
5 B
6 S
7 C
8 C
9 N

Giving instructions

A bank clerk is giving a customer instructions about where to write certain information on a form. Like this:

THE INFORMATION IS: 17 April 1982
THE CLERK SAYS: *Could you put it* in the place where it says 'date', please?

Could you put it is one of the phrases used on the opposite page to show people how to fill in a form.

Look at the other phrases you can use and then give similar instructions for the information listed below.

.... in the place where it says ....

1 0649973
2 Two £10 notes and three £5 notes
3 One 50p coin
4 Sidney Street, Oxford
5 *Kevin Whitman*
6 £35.50

Writing questions

Write questions using the following notes. Can you answer your questions?

1 What/you/give/bank/when/open/bank account?
2 How much/need/open/bank account/England?
3 What/example/signature/called?
4 What/pay/bank/services?
5 How/get/services/free/charge?

3 How to use a cheque book

A current account (American 'checking account') keeps your money safe. When you need cash or want to buy something or pay a bill, you can write a cheque in payment.

The name of the *payee* goes on the first line. If you want to withdraw money from the bank, just write CASH or SELF.

Your cheque book is personal to you. Each cheque is printed with your *name* and *account number.* (a/c no.)

The cheque is only valid if it is *dated* and your *signature* is in the bottom right-hand corner. It should be the same signature as the specimen you gave to the bank.

```
22/10/82
Grabbit &
Runne Ltd.
Old Balance    539·00
Deposits
Total          539·00
This Cheque    364·00
New Balance    175·00

654987
```

SHOESTRING BANK LIMITED
Morgantown Branch

PAY Grabbit & Runne Ltd
Three hundred and sixty-
four pounds only
P.M.

654987   01 01 01   03343473

01 01 0
DATE 28 October 19 8.
OR ORDER
£ 364.00p
PETER MOORE
Peter Moore

Each *cheque* has its own *number.*

Each bank branch has its own number called a *Bank Sort Code.*

Write the *amount* clearly in ink *in words and figures.* Begin writing as far to the left as possible. The bank has an obligation to honour the cheque if you have this amount of money in your account.

Keep a record of how much you have spent. Some cheque books have *stubs* or *counterfoils* on which you can write the details of your transaction.

Comprehension Choose the best answer.

1 A cheque is only valid when (a) the counterfoil is filled in (b) the payee is SELF (c) it is signed and dated by the account holder (d) the amount in words and figures is written in pencil.
2 A cheque with Pay CASH can be used by (a) the account holder to pay a bill (b) the account holder's friend at a bank (c) anyone anywhere (d) the account holder at a bank.

Finding the best word Fill in the missing words in each sentence. The words in brackets ( ) have the same meaning as the missing words.

1 You w . . . . money for yourself by writing CASH. (take out)
2 Henry had £100 in the bank. He spent £50 and paid in a cheque for £25. The b . . . . . . of his account was then £75.
3 Every time you make out a cheque, fill in the c . . . . (the small piece of paper at the side of the cheque)
4 An unsigned cheque is not v . . . . (you cannot use it)
5 Do not use a pencil to write a cheque. It must be written i . i . . (with a pen)

Numbers Below are six counterfoils which were filled in after the cheque had been written. Calculate the balance for each example. Write the amount in figures and then in words.

The first one has been done for you as an example.

Old Balance	£483.59	£220.37	£97.00	£1057.71	£428.62	£947.27
Deposits	22.87	—	22.12	197.00	504.48	387.50
Total	506.46					
This cheque	20.00	50.00	92.52	379.43	6.49	190.17
New Balance	1 486.46	2	3	4	5	6

REMEMBER! After the word 'hundred' you must say 'and'.
There is a hyphen (-) between the tens and the units (forty-four).

1 £486.46 Four hundred *and* eighty-six pounds, forty-six pence/p.
2 . . . .
3 . . . .
4 . . . .
5 . . . .
6 . . . .

Guided summary: Using a cheque book Write answers to these questions about how to use a cheque book, using the information on the opposite page.

1 What is each cheque printed with?
2 When is the cheque valid?
3 What do you write if you want to withdraw cash from the bank?
4 How should the amount be written?
5 Where can you keep a record of how much you have spent?
6 When does the bank have an obligation to honour the cheque?

4 Security

Since the days when the Wells Fargo stage coaches in North America were regularly attacked and robbed, banks have tried to develop systems of greater security.

As methods of payment have become more complex and sophisticated, so have the rules about how to use them.

TYPE OF PAYMENT	SECURITY SYSTEM
Cash—easy to steal 	1 Special armoured cars are used to carry money from bank to bank. 2 Banks have special rooms called vaults, where cash is kept. The Bank of England has no windows on the ground floor, and it is impossible to reach the USA's store of gold bullion at Fort Knox.
Cheques—can be forged 	1 They are only valid when signed and dated by the person whose name is printed on them. 2 If you make a mistake when writing a cheque you must cross it out and initial the correction. 3 If a crossed cheque is used, it can only be cashed by passing through the payee's bank account. ('Not negotiable' is sometimes written on the cheque for the same reason.) An open cheque can be cashed over the counter in a bank.
Cheque card—not worth stealing because it cannot be used alone as payment	1 It is used to guarantee a cheque. 2 The signature on the cheque card can be compared with the one on a cheque. 3 A cheque card is a guarantee to the payee that the bank will pay the amount on any cheque up to £50. For this reason you cannot stop a cheque which has the cheque card number on the back. 4 Cheques and cheque card should be kept separately.
Bank Giro slips—not worth stealing as they are not payment in themselves but only information about payment 	1 Bank Giro slips give the bank information about who you are paying and how much. You can fill in forms to: a) Pay money into your own account when you are not in your own branch. b) Pay money into another person's account. The form in the picture has been sent as a bill for rent from a housing company. Because a lot of people have to pay money to this company, they have bank giro credit slips ready printed with their name, address, account number and bank sort code. 2 You do not have to take cash or cheque all the way to your own bank. 3 No money travels from bank to bank—only the information.
Standing Order—nothing to be stolen	1 *Regular, fixed* payments like TV rental, can be paid by giving a Standing Order to your bank. 2 Money is automatically taken from your account but no cash changes hands.

The pickpocket's dream

The pickpocket found this cheque and cheque card in Mary Watkin's handbag. What a find!

True or false? Look at the statements below and tick (√) if you think they are true or false. Can you correct the false statements?

	TRUE	FALSE

1 Vaults are special armoured cars.
2 You can sign your own name on a cheque with someone else's name printed on it.
3 A cheque card can only be used with a cheque.
4 A crossed cheque can be cashed over the counter in a bank.
5 A Bank Giro slip is used for regular fixed payments.

Hidden word puzzle

Fill in the puzzle and find the missing word. Use these clues to help you.

Clues
1 Notes and coins
2 There are two kinds of cheques, crossed and ____
3 Complicated
4 Where customers are served in a bank
5 Regular payments are paid by standing ____
6 Not changing
7 Take without permission
8 The person who is paid

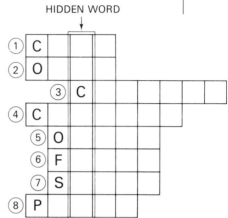

The pickpocket's dream

Look at the cheque in the pickpocket's hand on the page opposite. Last week Mary Watkins started to write out the cheque and then changed her mind. The pickpocket has just found it in her handbag.

1 Make a list of the things that the pickpocket has to do in order to take money from Mary's account.
2 Mary has made some serious mistakes in writing this cheque. Using SHOULD/SHOULD NOT in your answers, write some advice for Mary on how to fill in a cheque properly. (Unit 3 will help you too.)

Example: You should not sign a cheque before you have filled in all the other details.

Filling in a Bank Giro slip

Peter Moore wants to pay his rent to the Helga Housing Company. They bank at the Camden High Street branch of the Burlington Bank. He has lost their special Giro slip but can remember all the information which is on it.

Using this information and that from the Bank Giro slip on the opposite page, fill in the form below for Peter Moore. He pays in cash.

8

5 Your current account in operation

1 BUYING THINGS

A: That's £41.20 please.
B: *Will you take a cheque?*
A: Do you have any means of identification?
B: *Yes. I have a cheque card. Who shall I make the cheque payable to?*
A: Could you make it out to Miami Fashions Limited, please?
B: *There you are.*
A: Oh, you've put 31.20. Could you just change it to 41 please? And initial the correction.
B: *Certainly.*
A: Thank you very much, Mrs Dobbs. Here's your dress. Goodbye.

2 GETTING CASH

Do you need cash outside banking hours? If you have a current account ask your bank for a cash card. You can then use any of the cash dispensers which are outside our branches and in some large shops.

Opening Times:
8a.m.–9p.m. Monday–Saturday

Services:
Cash up to £100 (depending on the balance in your account)

A readout of your current account balance.

1 Put your cash card into the slot on the right-hand side of the machine. This opens the machine.

2 You will now see instructions in the personal viewer.

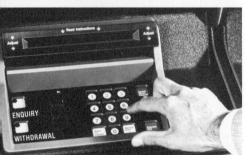

3 Tap in, on the buttons, your personal number, which the bank gave you with the card.

4 If you need a statement of your account, press 'enquiry'. You will see the balance in the viewer. If you need cash, press 'withdrawal' and the amount you need.

5 Press 'proceed' to tell the machine that you have finished.

6 The viewer shows you what you have asked for. If it is correct, press 'proceed'. If it is wrong, press 'cancel' and start again.

7 If you have asked for cash, the machine checks with a central computer that you have enough money in your account.

8 The machine gives back your card.

9 The machine counts your money and gives it to you.

10 Write on your record card how much you have withdrawn.

Comprehension Choose the best answer.

1 Mrs Dobbs is paying (a) by cheque (b) cash (c) by cash card (d) by cheque and cheque card.
2 To get cash outside banking hours you need (a) a cheque book (b) a cheque card (c) a cash card (d) a readout of your current balance.

Finding the best word Fill in the missing word in each sentence.

1 'Could you make the cheque p . . . . . . to' means the same as 'Could you make the cheque out to . . .'.
2 If you have a cash card and you need money outside banking hours, you should look for a cash d . . . .
3 The machine will tell you how much you have in your current account. This is called a r . . . . . . of your balance.
4 The hole where you put your cash card is called a s . . . .
5 T . . in, or press the right buttons for, your personal number.
6 If you want the machine to follow your instructions, you should press 'p . . . . . .'.
7 If you make a mistake, press 'c . . . . .'.

Instructions: Using the First Conditional Look at number 7 in the exercise above. Make sentences like this one using the information in columns A and B below. The information is mixed up, so you must find the correct answer before you can write the sentence.

	A	B
	you need cash	– you will see your balance in the viewer
	you press 'proceed'	– the machine checks with a central computer
IF	you ask for cash	– press 'enquiry'
	you put your cash card in the slot	– the viewer shows you what you have asked for
	you need a statement of your balance	– press 'withdrawal'
	you press 'enquiry'	– this will open the machine

Guided paragraph writing Look at the dialogue on the opposite page. Using the notes below, tell the story of Mrs Dobbs' visit to the shop. You should put the verbs in italics into the past simple tense and add any missing words.

Yesterday Mrs Dobbs *go*/Miami Fashions/buy/dress. It *cost* £41.20. She *pay*/cheque/cheque card and *make*/cheque/Miami Fashions Limited. By mistake/*write* £31.20 and/*have* to correct/initial/correction. The assistant *be* very helpful.

6 In the red!

SHOESTRING BANK LIMITED
7 The Parade, Morgantown, Clamshire.

In account with Shoestring Bank Ltd. Morgantown, Clamshire

0123456

MR AND MRS W DOBBS

Date	Detail	Debits	Credits	Balance ①
				33.42 O/D
19 SEP	BALANCE FORWARD	6.88		59.41 O/D
21 SEP	506932	25.99	⑤ 421.24	361.83
24 SEP	809254			236.23 ③
26 SEP	506935	125.60		36.23
3 OCT	CASH CARD	200.00		4.97 O/D
6 OCT	506937	41.20		22.57 O/D
11 OCT	506933	17.60		④ 102.57 O/D
20 OCT	506934	80.00		106.54 O/D
21 OCT	ACCOUNT CHARGE ⑥	3.97		

②

CUSTOMER: Good morning. I've called to pick up my monthly statement. Could you tell me if it's ready. Here's my account number. The name's Dobbs.

BANK CLERK: Here you are, Mr Dobbs.

CUSTOMER: Thank you very much.

CUSTOMER: Er. Excuse me. I think you've made a mistake. I should be about £500 in credit and I'm £117 in the red!

BANK CLERK: Just a moment Mr Dobbs. I'll go and check.

Yes. I see you have a joint account with your wife. She's drawn quite a lot of cheques on this account at Miami Fashions just lately. That's why your account is overdrawn. Perhaps you could have a word with her.

CUSTOMER: Yes, I can think of a very good one!

BUT IT WAS TOO LATE! A few days later, this letter arrived at the Dobbs' home.

SHOESTRING BANK LIMITED
7 The Parade, Morgantown, Clamshire

Mr and Mrs W Dobbs,
42 Spring Gardens,
Morgantown.

27 October 1982

Dear Mr and Mrs Dobbs,

A cheque for £46, signed by Mrs Dobbs, has been presented for payment by Miami Fashions. As the cheque was used with a cheque card, we have honoured it. However, your current account was already £106.54 overdrawn before this cheque was presented and you have an agreed limit of £120.

I would be very grateful if you could pay some money into your current account before using any more cheques. If you would like to increase your limit, I would be very happy to discuss this with you.

I enclose a statement.

Yours sincerely

J. Walker

J Walker
Branch manager

True or false? Look at the statements below and then tick (√) if you think they are true or false. Can you correct the false statements?

	TRUE	FALSE
1 At the end of the conversation, Mr Dobbs is angry.		
2 Mr and Mrs Dobbs have an agreed overdraft limit of £117.		
3 At the moment, their account is £153 overdrawn.		
4 The bank has not paid Miami Fashions.		

Finding the word *On the statement* opposite are some numbers in circles, like this: ①
Using the information in the dialogue, write the names of the things which are numbered.

1 the account is o . . . .
2 this paper is a s . . . .
3 the account is i . c . . . . .
4 the account is i . t . . r . .
5 a record of a c . . . . .
6 the money you pay to the bank to take care of your account is an a . . . . . . c . . . . .

The letter

1 I e . . . . . . a table of interest rates. (am sending with this letter)
2 My bank has said I can have an overdraft of £150 maximum. £150 is my a . . . . . l . . . .
3 If you begin 'Dear Mr' or 'Mrs' you end Y . . . . s . . . .
4 The word you put before a person's name at the beginning of a letter D . . .

Being polite Look again at the dialogue on the opposite page and in Unit 5. What do the people say when they:

1 want to ask someone politely to do something? (Unit 5)
2 give something to someone (Units 5 and 6)
3 ask for information (Unit 6)
4 ask someone to wait? (Unit 6)
5 reply to someone who asks them to do something? (Unit 5)

C . . . . y . . (j . . .) ———?
(T)H . . . y . . a . .
H . . .'s y . . . d . . . .
C . . . . y . . t . . m . ———?
J . . . a m . . . . .
C . . . .

Dialogue: At the bank
Finish this conversation. The numbers tell you which of the phrases from **Being polite** you can use.

You go into your bank to ask for the balance of your account.

CLERK: Good morning. Can I help you?
YOU: 3
CLERK: Could I have your account number please?
YOU: 5

You see that you have given the clerk your cheque card number by mistake. Ask him to wait and then give him the correct number.

YOU: 4
CLERK: Thank you.

The clerk goes away and returns with the balance on a piece of paper. He gives it to you.

CLERK: 2
YOU: Thank you. Goodbye.

12

7 Credit cards

ACCORD

You cannot afford to be without a credit card in today's busy world. An ACCORD card offers you the following advantages:

★ Many shops and restaurants throughout the country accept our card as payment
★ No interest charged if money repaid within 2 months
★ Personal credit limit—minimum £100
★ Cash advance of £100 per day
★ Minimum monthly repayment—10% per month
★ Additional cards on your account for anyone over 18

SHOESTRINGER

Let Shoestringer do the job

Why carry cash? Shoestringer acts as a credit card and a cheque card too. It can be used in shops, restaurants, airports, garages, not only in this country but abroad as well. We do not charge interest on your Shoestringer account for up to a month and we send you a monthly statement to remind you how much you have spent. If an unauthorized person uses your card without your permission, the most money we would ask you to pay us (the maximum liability) is only £25.

FLEXICARD

MORE USEFUL THAN CASH..........

FLEXICARD
000 932 02498761
MRS P MANSFIELD

AND SAFER!!!

- minimum monthly repayments 5%
- £50 cash a day
- 1 month interest free
- additional cards
- used nationwide
- £200 credit limit

Using a credit card

CONVERSATION 1

MAN: Have you got 2 balcony seats for Thursday 31st?
WOMAN: Hold the line please.... Yes sir. That'll be £10 for the two.
MAN: Thank you. My Accord number's 90371528.

CONVERSATION 2

MAN: Now, 4 days' hire comes to £56, madam.
WOMAN: Can I pay by Flexicard?
MAN: Yes, that's fine. Here are the keys.

CONVERSATION 3

WOMAN: Here's the ticket you booked, sir. They've just called your flight.
MAN: Do you take Shoestringer?
WOMAN: Yes.... Just sign here please.... Have a pleasant flight.

| | Reading comprehension | Complete the table for Accord, Shoestringer and Flexicard using the information opposite. Put a — if the information is not given in the advertisements (see examples). |

WHAT DIFFERENT CREDIT CARDS CAN OFFER YOU

	ACCORD	SHOESTRINGER	FLEXICARD	YOUR CARD
1 use all over the country		YES		
2 use abroad			YES	
3 agreed credit limit				£200
4 cash per day		—		
5 monthly statements	—			
6 interest-free period			1 month	
7 use as a cheque card				—
8 additional cards		—		
9 maximum liability	—			
10 minimum monthly repayment			—	

Finding the best word

Fill in the missing word in each sentence.

1 A p....... credit limit is especially arranged for each person.
2 'A......' is another word for 'loan'.
3 M...... repayments are paid every 30 days.
4 If someone else wants to use your account, he needs an .... card.
5 A..... is another way of saying 'in another country'.
6 We do not c..... (make you pay) for this service.
7 An .... person is someone who does not have permission to do something.
8 M...... is the opposite of minimum.
9 The money you would have to pay if you lost your credit card is your l......... .
10 N......... means all over the country.

Structure practice: Present tenses Using a credit card

Look at the three short conversations on the opposite page and answer the following questions in complete sentences.

Conversation 1
a) Who is the man talking to?
b) What does he want?

Conversation 2
a) Where is the woman?
b) What is she doing?
c) What is her question?

Conversation 3
a) Where is the man?
b) What is he paying for?
c) What is his question?

Guided summary

Find an advertisement for a real credit card. Fill in the information in column 4 in the first exercise on this page. Now write a paragraph about the advantages (and disadvantages, if any,) of using this particular card. Use the examples on the opposite page to help you.

8 Borrowing money

Mr Dobbs was really worried! He wanted to buy a new car but his current account was always overdrawn. One day, when he went in to see the bank manager, he saw this notice on the wall.

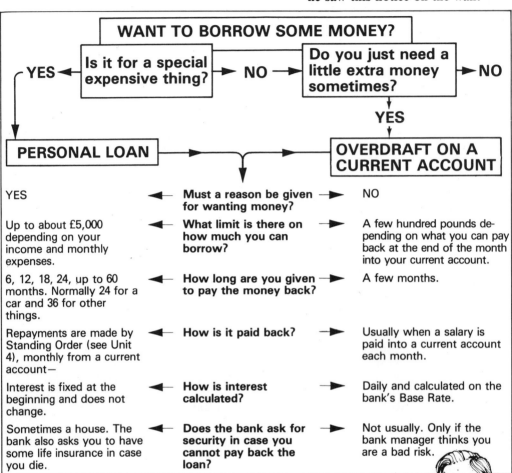

WANT TO BORROW SOME MONEY?

- Is it for a special expensive thing? **YES** → PERSONAL LOAN
- **NO** → Do you just need a little extra money sometimes?
  - **YES** → OVERDRAFT ON A CURRENT ACCOUNT
  - **NO**

PERSONAL LOAN	Question	OVERDRAFT ON A CURRENT ACCOUNT
YES	Must a reason be given for wanting money?	NO
Up to about £5,000 depending on your income and monthly expenses.	What limit is there on how much you can borrow?	A few hundred pounds depending on what you can pay back at the end of the month into your current account.
6, 12, 18, 24, up to 60 months. Normally 24 for a car and 36 for other things.	How long are you given to pay the money back?	A few months.
Repayments are made by Standing Order (see Unit 4), monthly from a current account—	How is it paid back?	Usually when a salary is paid into a current account each month.
Interest is fixed at the beginning and does not change.	How is interest calculated?	Daily and calculated on the bank's Base Rate.
Sometimes a house. The bank also asks you to have some life insurance in case you die.	Does the bank ask for security in case you cannot pay back the loan?	Not usually. Only if the bank manager thinks you are a bad risk.

PAYING BACK A PERSONAL LOAN

Here is a table of different loans and the monthly repayments depending on the period of the loan. The bank manager is explaining to a customer how the personal loan system works.

	Amount of loan	300	1250	2350	3000
12 MTHS	Total amount £	332.87	1386.79*	2607.14	3328.23
	Monthly repayments £	27.73	115.56	217.25	277.35
18 MTHS	Total amount £	*348.73	1452.89	2731.38	3486.85
	Monthly repayments £	19.37	80.71	151.74	193.71
24 MTHS	Total amount £	365.04	1520.86	2859.12	3649.93
	Monthly repayments £	15.21	63.36	119.13	152.08
30 MTHS	Total amount £	381.84	1590.63	*2990.40	3817.49
	Monthly repayments £	12.72	53.02	99.68	127.24
36 MTHS	Total amount £	399.07	1662.48	3125.34	*3989.82
	Monthly repayments £	11.08	46.18	86.81	110.82

If you borrow £1,250 (one thousand, two hundred and fifty pounds) and pay it back over 12 (twelve) months, the total amount payable is £1,386.79 (one thousand, three hundred and eighty-six pounds, seventy-nine p), the interest is £136.79 (a hundred and thirty-six pounds seventy nine p) and you make 12 (twelve) monthly repayments of £115.56p (a hundred and fifteen pounds fifty-six p).

True or false? Look at the statements below and then tick (√) if you think they are true or false. Can you correct the false statements?

	TRUE	FALSE
1 The bank always asks for some security if you want an overdraft.		
2 If you want to borrow money to buy a boat, you ask the bank for a personal loan.		
3 The rate of interest on a personal loan changes depending on the bank's Base Rate.		
4 An overdraft is money borrowed from a current account.		
5 Everyone can get a loan of £5,000.		

Finding the best word Fill in the spaces using words from the texts opposite. The words in brackets ( ) have the same meaning as the missing words.

1 D . . . . means every day.
2 The rate of interest is f . . . . (it doesn't change)
3 Have you read the n . . . . . on the wall about new interest rates?
4 An e . . . . thing is one which costs a lot of money.
5 If you can't pay back a loan, the bank will lose a lot of money. To stop this, the bank asks if you have some s . . . ., for example your house, which could be sold to pay off the loan.
6 The loan is £200, the interest is £21.91, so you give us 12 monthly r . . . . of £18.49.

Numbers Look at the table of loans on the opposite page. Write out sentences for the numbers marked * like this:

If you borrow ——— and pay it back over . . . . months, the total amount payable is . . . ., the interest is . . . . and you make . . . . monthly payments of . . . .

Write out the numbers in words.

Guided writing: Second Conditional sentences Look at this sentence and notice how it is formed.

If I wanted to buy a car, I would ask for a personal loan.

If + past simple, ... , would + infinitive without *to* . . . . . .

Make similar sentences using the notes below. For each one say if you would ask for a personal loan or an overdraft.

1 (need) 18 months for repayment
2 (have) no security
3 (want) a fixed interest rate
4 (need) a little extra money sometimes
5 (want) to borrow £2,000

9 Deposit accounts and investment

What's the difference between a current account and a deposit account?

Well, to put it simply, a current account is used for handling day-to-day finances, whereas a deposit account is really for saving money. That's why children can open one.

So an adult can have both then?

Yes, that's right. In fact, you can save regularly by transferring a certain sum every month from your current account to your deposit account, where it can earn interest. You can do this by standing order.

How does a deposit account work?

Well, when you open the account, we give you a paying-in book. With this you can deposit money at any branch, but if you don't have it with you, you can use one of the branch's Bank Giro credit slips.

And what about when I want to take money out of my account?

Then you use a withdrawal slip. But don't forget to give us a week's notice. If you want money immediately, you lose some interest.

Are deposit accounts a good form of investment?

For the short-term saver, yes. If you can leave your money with us for a longer period, like 6 months, you could open a Special Savings Account.

Why is it special?

Well, as we have your money for a minimum of six months we pay you interest at 1% above normal rate or Base Rate, which is fixed by the Bank of England.

What about other kinds of investment?

This is very complicated. It depends on how much money you want to invest and for how long. Also it's possible to *lose* money with some forms of investment, whereas deposit and savings accounts are safe. Generally, the greater the risk, the bigger the return. Now, if you tell me a little more about your finances, I'll try to advise you.

True or false? Look at the statements below and tick (√) if you think they are true or false. Can you correct the false statements?

	TRUE	FALSE
1 A deposit account is the same as a current account.		
2 A current account is used for handling day-to-day finances.		
3 When paying money into your deposit account you can only do it by using a paying-in book.		
4 The normal or Base Rate of interest is fixed by the Bank of England.		

Using the right expression Choose the best answer.

1 If you want to move money from your current to your deposit account, you (a) withdraw it (b) pay it out (c) transfer it (d) save it.
2 The best way to do this regularly is by (a) cheque (b) paying-in slip (c) paying-in book (d) standing order.
3 You should give a week's notice before using (a) a cheque (b) a credit slip (c) a withdrawal slip (d) a standing order.
4 A good form of investment for the short-term saver is (a) a current account (b) a standing order (c) a Special Savings Account (d) a deposit account.

Comparing alternatives There are several differences between a current account and a deposit account. Look at this sentence from the first dialogue opposite.

'....... a current account is used for handling your day-to-day finances, *whereas* a deposit account is really for saving money.'

Complete the following sentences using *whereas*.

1 Only adults can use current accounts ....
2 Your money does not earn interest in a current account ....
3 You use cheques to take money out of a current account.........
4 With a current account you do not have to give notice of withdrawal..

Asking questions A friend is asking you about ways of investing money with a bank. Write his questions from the notes and then answer them.

Example: What/difference/current account/deposit account?
Q: What is the difference between a current account and a deposit account?
A: A current account is for day-to-day finances and a deposit account is for saving money.

Now do the same with these questions. Use the dialogue opposite to help you.

1 Which form/use/withdraw money/deposit account?
2 Which form/use/pay money in?
3 How much notice/give/before/withdraw money?
4 How/move money/current account/deposit account?
5 What/good form/investment/short-term saver?
6 What rate/interest/get/Special Savings Account?

10 Running a business

SHOESTRING BANK LIMITED

7 The Parade,
Morgantown,
Clamshire

Our Ref: JW/GB

E L Adams, Esq.,
Adams Flower Shop,
69 High Street,
Morgantown.

22 December 1982

Dear Mr Adams,

Thank you very much for your letter of 15 December, telling us about your expansion plans and enquiring about a Business Expansion Loan. I enclose a copy of our guide to the features and conditions of the loan.

I should perhaps explain one point in the guide - the idea of a capital repayment 'holiday'. This means that you may not have to repay any of the capital during the first two years. This will clearly help you in the early stages of the expansion of your business.

I hope this information is useful to you. The other questions in your letter are more difficult to answer directly. Might I suggest that we meet to discuss these matters? Perhaps you would be kind enough to telephone to arrange a suitable time. I will need up-to-date information on your sales figures and order books to advise you properly. I would be grateful if you would send me these figures before our meeting so that I can prepare myself.

If you need any more information, please do not hesitate to contact me.

Yours sincerely

J. Walker

J Walker
Branch manager

Business Expansion Loan

PURPOSE To allow expansion through purchase of capital assets or another business

WHAT QUALIFIES FOR A LOAN? Established, profitable businesses wishing to expand e.g. sole traders, partnerships and private companies

SIZE OF LOAN £5,000 – £500,000

TERM 2 – 20 years

METHOD OF CHARGING Interest on balance, either a variable or a fixed rate

CAPITAL REPAYMENT Monthly but with possible 2 year capital 'holiday' repayment at start

BENEFITS (1) Opportunities for capital repayment 'holiday' (2) Choice of interest options (3) Up to 20 year term

Comprehension Choose the best answer and say why the others are wrong.

1 Mr Adams is planning to (a) start a business (b) buy a business (c) expand his business (d) sell his business.
2 The bank manager has written him a letter to (a) explain the Business Expansion Loan guide (b) answer all his questions (c) offer him a loan (d) suggest a meeting.
3 Before the meeting Mr Adams must telephone the bank to (a) arrange a time to meet (b) send some figures (c) advise the bank manager (d) prepare himself.

Hidden word puzzle

Fill in the puzzle and find the missing word.

Clues
1 A project
2 A formal way of saying 'buy'
3 Money which is lent
4 Another word for 'numbers'
5 To give advice
6 Most recent
7 The opposite of public: a _____ company
8 Some interest is at a fixed rate and some is at a _____ rate
9 Happening once every month
10 A period of time: the _____ of the loan

HIDDEN WORD

(1) P
(2) P
(3) L
(4) F
(5) A
(6) U — —
(7) P
(8) V
(9) M
(10) T

Being formal Look at the letter from the bank manager to Mr Adams. He uses some formal polite expressions because it is a business letter. What expressions does he use to say the following things more formally?

1 Thanks a lot.
2 I'm sending ....
3 Let me tell you about ....
4 Why don't we .....
5 Please phone.
6 I want you to ....
7 Get in touch with me if you like.

Letter writing Using the expressions from the last exercise and the following information, write a letter to the bank manager, Mr Walker.

To: (take the name and address from the letter opposite)

First paragraph: Thank him for his letter.
   Tell him you are sending the information he asked for.

Second paragraph: Thank him for his offer of a meeting.
   Apologise for not telephoning. You have been away for Christmas (I am extremely sorry for ....)
   Tell him you are coming into the bank next Monday.
   Suggest that you arrange a time for the meeting then.
   If he is not free, ask him to give his secretary a note of suitable times.

Third paragraph: Tell him you look forward to seeing him.
Thank him for his help.

You began 'Dear Mr Walker'. How should you finish?

11 Foreign exchange

Exchange Rates
16 February 1981

	WE BUY NOTES	TRAVELLERS CHEQUES	WE SELL NOTES
AUSTRIA (schillings)	37.25	35.9	35.25
BELGIUM (francs)	84.5	82.0	80.5
CANADA (dollars)	2.78	2.72	2.7
DENMARK (krone)	16.0	15.46	15.35
FRANCE (francs)	11.93	11.68	11.48
GERMANY (deutschmarks)	5.19	5.07	4.97
GREECE (drachma)	119.00	118.00	113.00
HOLLAND (guilders)	5.64	5.5	5.39
ITALY (lire)	2510.00	2389.00	2410.00
NORWAY (kroner)	13.08	12.52	12.48
PORTUGAL (escudos)	134.00	131.5	127.00
SPAIN (pesetas)	202.00	200.75	194.00
SWEDEN (kronor)	11.06	10.7	10.56
SWITZERLAND (francs)	4.76	4.635	4.53
USA (dollars)	2.315	2.28	2.24
YUGOSLAVIA (dinar)	87.00	_____	83.00

These rates may not necessarily apply for large amounts or for notes of large denominations.
Commission charges per currency: notes sold by bank 50p
foreign notes bought 40p
travellers cheques £1 per person

Fixing the Exchange Rate

Foreign exchange rates change every day. On the London Foreign Exchange (FX) market, they are fixed by dealers from over 200 banks round the world who buy and sell money by telephone. The 'price' of a country's currency depends on many different things including:

- the economic and political situation in that country
- the amount of control that a government has over the currency. (For example it can limit how much money is allowed out of the country. This is called Exchange Control.)

The price of currency can change dramatically. In 1976 an Italian had to pay 1,491 lire for £1 sterling. On February 16, 1981 (see above) he had to pay 2,510 lire.

The Foreign Exchange always quotes two prices for each currency. A selling price and a buying price. For example:

US $2.2915 — $2.2925
selling rate   buying rate

Banks always SELL LOW — BUY HIGH. Do you understand why?

True or false? Look at the sentences below and tick (√) if you think they are true or false. Can you correct the false statements?

	TRUE	FALSE
1 The exchange rate for 20,000 Swiss francs may be different from the exchange rates given in the list on the wall of the bank.		
2 It does not cost anything to cash a travellers cheque.		
3 The price of a currency does not change very much.		
4 Can you answer the question at the bottom of p. 21?		

Word puzzle

You can find words hidden horizontally, vertically and diagonally in this puzzle. Use the clues to help you find the words. The first one has been done for you.

1 Country which uses lire.
2 The currency in Portugal
3 What the bank charges for changing one currency into another
4 The country where guilders come from
5 One of the countries which uses dollars
6 A Scandinavian country
7 If you are only allowed to take a limited amount of money out of your country this is an exchange ____
8 Greece's currency
9 Where dinars come from
10 A person who buys and sells money
11 Currency prices are ____ on the FX

B	C	A	E	S	C	U	D	O	S	N	Z
Y	Q	L	R	C	O	N	T	R	O	L	P
T	M	S	P	R	M	H	I	K	I	H	J
D	R	A	C	H	M	A	X	T	W	O	F
E	E	S	D	Q	I	N	D	W	A	L	S
N	B	Y	I	U	S	N	E	G	U	L	P
M	Y	U	G	O	S	L	A	V	I	A	Y
A	P	I	C	T	I	A	L	R	D	N	E
R	A	L	E	E	O	R	E	S	Q	D	U
K	O	T	E	D	N	E	R	X	C	H	A

Calculating exchange rates

Using the table of exchange rates in an English bank on 16th February 1981 (see opposite page), calculate the following:

1 An Austrian goes into the bank with Austrian travellers cheques. What do £10 sterling cost, excluding commission?
2 You have $100 in American travellers cheques. How much will the bank give you in pounds sterling after commission?
3 You are in England and have £100 to buy some Swiss francs. How many will you get after commission?
4 Two friends return from Belgium and Holland with 1700 Belgian francs and 28 guilders each. They change them into pounds sterling. How much do they have together in pounds when they walk out of the bank? How could they have saved some money?

Guided summary: Foreign exchange rates

Look at the information opposite. Answer the following questions in full sentences. Your answers should make a paragraph. Begin each answer with the words in brackets.

1 Who fixes foreign exchange rates? (Dealers from . . . .)
2 How often do these rates change? (These rates . . . .)
3 What often depends on the economic and political situation amongst other things? (The 'price' . . . .)
4 How many prices does the Foreign Exchange always quote? (The Foreign Exchange always . . .)
5 How do banks always sell and buy? (Banks always . . . .)

12 Ordering travellers cheques and foreign currency

TELEPHONIST:	Shoestring Bank. Good morning.
MR WATSON:	Oh, Good morning. I'd like to order some foreign currency and some travellers cheques please.
TELEPHONIST:	Hold the line please.
	....
CLERK:	Can I help you?
MR W:	Yes. I'd like to order some foreign currency and travellers cheques please.
CLERK:	Do you have an account at this branch, sir?
MR W:	Yes. My name's Watson, D L Watson. My account is – just a moment – er – 02468391.
CLERK:	Thank you. I'll deal with the travellers cheques first. Would you prefer them in pounds sterling or in dollars?
MR W:	Dollars please.
CLERK:	They come in $20, $50, $100 and $500 denominations.
MR W:	I'll take ten 50s please.
CLERK:	And you'd like some currency?
MR W:	Yes. I'm going to Scandinavia, Germany and the Netherlands, so I'd better take £20 worth of each of Swedish and Norwegian kronor, Belgian francs, guilders and deutschmarks.
CLERK:	Right. Well, that's £100 worth of currency and $500 in travellers cheques. Shall I debit your account?
MR W:	Yes, please.
CLERK:	And when would you like them?
MR W:	I'm leaving on 20th June, so I'd better pick them up the day before. That's in 3 days. Is that enough notice?
CLERK:	Yes, sir. That will be fine. Could I have your telephone number and I'll call you when they're ready.
MR W:	Yes. It's 01-468-4083.
CLERK:	Thank you. Goodbye.
MR W:	Goodbye.

TRAVELLERS CHEQUES AND FOREIGN CURRENCY ORDER FORM

Please supply travellers cheques and currency as shown below for collection on [19] Please allow at least three working days before collection date.

TRAVELLERS CHEQUES

QUANTITY	VALUE	QUANTITY	VALUE
	at £10		at $20
	at £20		at $50
	at £50		at $100
	at £100		at $500
Total Value £		Total Value $	

FOREIGN CURRENCY

Austria	£	Portugal	£
Belgium	£	Spain	£
France	£	Sweden	£
Greece	£	Switzerland	£
Holland	£	USA	£
Italy	£	W. Germany	£
Norway	£	Yugoslavia	£
		Other	£

TICK BOX

I will pay by Shoestringer ☐
I will pay cash ☐
Please debit my account no. _____

Name
Address
Daytime telephone number
Signature   Date

Comprehension Look at the form at the bottom of the opposite page. When Mr Watson phoned the bank to order his travellers cheques and currency, the clerk filled in the details on this form.

Read the dialogue and fill in all the details of Mr Watson's order.

Choosing the right word Choose the best word to fit the definition.

1 The particular kind of money used in a country.
   (a) cash   (b) travellers cheques   (c) notes   (d) currency
2 How much a cheque is worth is its _____
   (a) quantity   (b) currency   (c) value   (d) cheque
3 When the bank takes money out of your account, it _____ your account.
   (a) debits   (b) withdraws   (c) transfers   (d) pays in
4 Information or warning that something is going to happen.
   (a) order   (b) denomination   (c) notice   (d) collection
5 You can buy American Express travellers cheques in _____ of 20, 50, 100, and 500 dollars.
   (a) currency   (b) quantity   (c) denominations   (d) debits

Changing reported speech into direct speech Below are 10 sentences *reporting* what the clerk and Mr Watson said to each other when Mr Watson ordered his travellers cheques. From the dialogue on the opposite page, can you find the five questions and five statements with the actual words they used?

Questions
1 The clerk asked Mr Watson if he could help him.
2 The clerk asked Mr Watson if he had an account at that branch.
3 The clerk asked Mr Watson if he would like some currency too.
4 The clerk asked Mr Watson if he should debit his account.
5 The clerk asked Mr Watson when he would like the currency and cheques.

Statements
1 Mr Watson said that he would like to order some foreign currency.
2 He said that his name was Watson.
3 The clerk said that he would deal with the travellers cheques first.
4 Mr Watson said that he would take ten 50s.
5 Mr Watson said that he was leaving on 20th June.

Dialogue writing Below is another form for ordering foreign currency and travellers cheques. The lady telephoned the bank last week and the clerk took down the details on this form. Using the dialogue on the opposite page to help you, write the conversation which took place.

TRAVELLERS CHEQUES AND FOREIGN CURRENCY ORDER FORM

Please supply travellers cheques and currency as shown below for collection on **24 March 1981**. Please allow at least three working days before collection date.

TRAVELLERS CHEQUES				FOREIGN CURRENCY			
QUANTITY	VALUE	QUANTITY	VALUE	Austria	£	Portugal	£ **15**
	at £10		at $20	Belgium	£	Spain	£ **15**
5	at £20 **£100**		at $50	France	£	Sweden	£
4	at £50 **£200**		at $100	Greece	£	Switzerland	£
	at £100		at $500	Holland	£	USA	£
				Italy	£	W. Germany	£
Total Value **£300**		Total Value $		Norway	£	Yugoslavia	£
		TICK BOX				Other	£

I will pay by Shoestringer ☐   Name **MISS MARY PARKER**
I will pay cash ☐   Address **62 HIGH STREET, MORGANTOWN**
Please debit my account no. **04968288**   Daytime telephone number **Morgantown 28631**
Signature _____   Date **18 March 1981**

24

13 What do you do if you need money in other countries?

TRAVELLERS CHEQUES

Joan and Peter Robinson

'We took travellers cheques to Ibiza on our holiday last summer. They're so quick and safe. You sign them all once in the bank where you buy them. When you want to cash them, all you do is countersign and date them and use your passport as identification. The foreign bank calculates their value in local currency, using the daily exchange rates and takes a small commission or encashment charge. You keep a record of the serial numbers and which ones you've already cashed on the form they give you. If the rest are stolen, you telex your bank at home, give them the serial numbers, and usually they will be able to give you replacement cheques or cash on the next business day.'

TRAVELLERS CHEQUES

DRAWERS ENDORSEMENT (DATE) _____

Shoestring Bank Limited
71 Haywood St., London EC3

$50

Pay Self or Order

FIFTY Dollars
or the equivalent abroad
at current rates of exchange

Valid in all countries of the World unless otherwise endorsed

SIGNATURE OF DRAWER
06589212

RECORD OF ENCASHMENTS

DATE CASHED	WHERE CASHED	Record serial numbers (need be only last 3 figures) under appropriate denomination.			
		$10	$20	$50	$100
20/6	Skandinaviska Enskilda Banken		026489		
22/6	Hotel Kramer, Malmo, Sweden		490	069801	
23/6	Deutsche Bank, Hamburg				096342
26/6	Hotel Atlantic, Hamburg				943
26/6	Lufthansa				944
27/7	Bloch Department Store, Brussels		491		
27/7	Banque Nationale, Brussels		492	802	
28/7	Channel Ferries, Hook of Holland		493		

EUROCHEQUES

Cornelia Westphal

'When I travel to other European countries on business, I use normal cheques from my German bank, both for getting cash from the bank and for paying in shops and hotels. With one of these Eurocheques, I simply fill in the currency of the country I'm in and the amount, show my cheque guarantee card and sign the cheque in the usual way. In some countries, such as Britain, however, only banks accept Eurocheques. They must be written in Deutschmarks and are then converted into pounds sterling like a travellers cheque.'

OPEN CREDIT

Pietro Langnese

'I'm an engineer and often work in Bahrain for two or three months at a time. I find the easiest way of getting money here is with an open credit arrangement. My bank at home sends a copy of my signature to a specified bank in Bahrain. Then I can cash my cheques, up to an agreed limit, just the same as at home.'

True or false? Look at the sentences below and tick (√) if you think they are true or false. Can you correct the false statements?

	TRUE	FALSE

1 If you want to open credit arrangements at a foreign bank, you give that bank a copy of your signature.
2 If you have open credit at a foreign bank you can withdraw as much money as you like.
3 Open credit is best for people travelling from country to country.
4 Eurocheques are different from the normal cheques issued by banks in Europe.
5 Eurocheques can only be used to withdraw money from a bank.
6 A German Eurocheque can be written out in guilders in a Belgian shop.
7 When you buy travellers cheques, you sign them when the bank clerk gives them to you.
8 If you lose your travellers cheques when you are abroad, you will probably have to return home.

Hidden word puzzle

Fill in the puzzle and find the missing word. Use these clues to help you.

Clues
1 Encashment ——— or commission
2 Works out
3 Fixed previously
4 Changed
5 Each cheque has its own ——— number
6 Taken without your permission
7 Sign again
8 Secure, not dangerous
9 Substitute

HIDDEN WORD ↓

1 C
2 C
3 A
4 C
5 S
6 S
7 C
8 S
9 R

Using your travellers cheques
Look at the Record of Encashments slip on the opposite page. Write a summary of how Mr Watson spent his travellers cheques, like this:

On 26 June, he paid his bill at the Hotel Atlantic with a $100 cheque, serial number (no.) 096943.

Writing a dialogue: Cashing a travellers cheque
Using the information opposite and the politeness phrases from Unit 6, complete the dialogue between Mary Parker (Unit 12) and the Spanish bank clerk who cashed her travellers cheques.

CLERK: (help?)
MARY: (cash cheques for $120)
CLERK: (countersign and ......)
MARY: (gives the cheques to the
      : clerk)
CLERK: (passport?)
MARY: (gives him the passport)

CLERK: (wait a moment ....
CLERK: (10,440 pesetas.
       100 pesetas encashment)
       (gives her a receipt)
MARY: (........)

14 Sending money abroad

If you want to send money abroad, you can do it in several different ways.

METHOD OF SENDING	TYPE OF CURRENCY (from Britain)	CHARGES	SENDER/METHOD	TIME	MUST THE MONEY GO THROUGH A BANK ACCOUNT?
International Money Order	£ St. up to £500 US up to $1,000	Remitter pays small service charge. Beneficiary pays exchange commission.	The remitter sends personally by letter.	Remitter receives IMO immediately. Period to other country depends on post.	No. Beneficiary can identify himself and receive cash over the counter.
Foreign Draft	£ St. or any foreign currency	Remitter pays service and exchange charge if draft is in foreign currency. Charges larger than for IMO.	The remitter sends personally by letter. IMO is more widely used now.	If draft is in foreign currency remitter receives after several days. Period to other country depends on post.	Yes.
International Money Transfer	£ St. or any foreign currency	Remitter usually pays all service and exchange charges. This type of payment is often used by businesses.	The remitter's bank transfers money to a bank in the foreign country. By airmail.	Several days depending on post.	No. It can be direct to the beneficiary, to his account or be used to open an account in his name.
Telegraphic or Cable Transfer	£ St. or any foreign currency	There are home bank, foreign bank and cable charges. The remitter usually pays the first two. This method is quite expensive.	The same as for IMT but by telegraph for speed.	24 hours	No. It can be direct to the beneficiary, to his account or be used to open an account in his name.

Sending money from one country to another is a complicated business. The following diagram shows how it is done.

ENGLAND

① REMITTER JEFF WALL → SHOESTRING BANK, THE PARADE, MORGANTOWN: 'I would like to send £20 to Dieter Schmidt at Deutsche Bank, Hamburg. Please debit my account and send by IMT.'

② SHOESTRING BANK → SHOESTRING INTERNATIONAL LONDON: 'Debit our A/C by £20 and transfer to Dieter Schmidt, Hamburg.'

③ SHOESTRING INTERNATIONAL LONDON → DEUTSCHE BANK INTERNATIONAL (Shoestring International have an A/C here in DM): 'Convert £20 into DM at today's rate of exchange and debit our account. Send to Dieter Schmidt, Hamburg.'

④ DEUTSCHE BANK INTERNATIONAL → DEUTSCHE BANK, ALSTER ALLEE, HAMBURG: 'Here is 102 DM. Please credit Dieter Schmidt.'

⑤ DEUTSCHE BANK → BENEFICIARY DIETER SCHMIDT: 'We have 102 DM for you from Jeff Wall.' 'Thank you.'

GERMANY

Comprehension
1 I want to send some money urgently to my sister in Rome. Her travellers cheques have been stolen. How shall I send it?
2 What is the cheapest way for me to send some money to my nephew in Canada for his birthday?
3 Can I send an International Money Order from England in Brazilian cruzeiros?
4 Smith Brothers Ltd need to pay some money to Kjendlie Exports in Oslo. How do you think they will pay?
5 I want to pay a deposit to a hotel in Amsterdam for my holiday in July. I'd like to send a letter giving them the details. Which are the best ways of doing it?

Choosing the right word
1 The person who wishes to send the money is the (a) dealer (b) beneficiary (c) receiver (d) remitter.
2 The person who receives the money is the (a) dealer (b) beneficiary (c) remitter (d) sender.
3 Please can you open an account _____ the name of Mohammed Shawash. (a) for (b) under (c) in (d) to
4 If the bank clerk asks you to _____ yourself, you must show him your passport. (a) credit (b) sign (c) honour (d) identify

Talking about how systems work 1

The diagram opposite shows how Jeff Wall sends money to Dieter Schmidt in Germany. Using the verbs from the list, complete the description of how money is transferred from one country to another. When we are talking about how systems work, we say for example:

'The money *is sent*'. (We use the passive form of the verb.)

transfer, convert, withdraw, fill in, inform, debit, send, credit, collect.

When someone goes to his bank and asks to send money abroad, for example to Austria, he first has to pay the money to the bank. He either pays in cash or his account _____. All the details of payment _____ on an International Money Transfer form and the money _____ from his local branch to the International Headquarters of his bank. A letter enclosing the Money Transfer form _____ to the International Headquarters of an Austrian bank. The amount in sterling _____ into schillings and that number of schillings _____ from the English bank's Austrian account. The Austrian money _____ to the beneficiary's account at his local branch. The beneficiary _____ and the money _____.

Guided writing: Writing questions

Look at this example.

QUESTION: How long does an International Money Transfer take?
ANSWER: Several days depending on the post.

Now, in the same way, make *questions* for the following answers.

1 24 hours
2 The remitter sends the money personally by letter.
3 No. The beneficiary can identify himself and receive cash over the counter.
4 The remitter pays a small service charge and the beneficiary pays the exchange commission.
5 By telegraph.

15 A day in the life of the bank

The Morgantown branch of the Shoestring Bank has a staff of eight.

```
                    MANAGER
                       |
                   CHIEF CLERK
   _____|_____
   |          |          |          |         |          |
SENIOR OR  JUNIOR    TYPIST/    COMPUTER   CASHIER   CASHIER
SECURITIES CLERK     CLERK      OPERATOR
CLERK
```

There is a lot of work to be done during the day and the staff in a small branch have to be able to do many different jobs. Here is a plan of a typical day:

TIME	8.30 a.m.	9.00	9.30 Bank opens		3.30 Bank closes	4.30–5.00
MANAGER			Open the safe.	The manager reads his letters and dictates replies. He has interviews with customers and often leaves the branch during the day to visit customer's offices and look round their businesses. While he is away, the chief clerk is in charge.		
CHIEF CLERK				The chief clerk organises work for the staff. He takes over from the manager when he is out of the office. He is responsible for staff training and helps and advises the staff. He also does the accounting.	Organises work for staff.	
SENIOR or SECURITIES CLERK	2 members of staff arrive and open the bank. The staff take turns at this. They open incoming mail and sort it.	The rest of the staff arrive.	The night safe is emptied and the contents checked. The cash dispenser balances are checked and the machine is refilled with cash. Cheques from the central clearing system are checked.	The senior or securities clerk handles the difficult paperwork. He often handles the problems which need expert knowledge, such as wills, loans and securities and foreign business.	Finish 'business of day'. Sometimes meet to discuss important problems or other matters.	Staff leave.
COMPUTER OPERATOR				The computer operator enters all the customers' credits and debits through the computer terminal.		
TYPIST/ CLERK			The typist deals with the mail.	The typist types the branch's letters and also handles the enquiries at the counter. She is responsible for Standing Orders.	Organises outgoing mail.	
JUNIOR CLERK			The cashiers collect the cash for their tills from the safe.	The junior clerk has general duties. He works on the counter during busy times, handling statements and the telephone. The junior clerk is usually the 'waste clerk' (see Unit 16).	Clear desks and balance cash. Return cash from till to safe.	
CASHIERS				The cashiers work at the counter, taking in and paying out money (including foreign transactions in a small bank). They also give out statements.		

True or false? Look at the sentences below and tick (√) if you think they are true or false. Can you correct the false statements?

	TRUE	FALSE
1 Each member of staff in a small branch is a specialist who only does one job.		
2 All the staff of the Morgantown branch arrive together.		
3 The chief clerk is second-in-command to the manager.		
4 The cashiers open the safe.		
5 The typist is responsible for enquiries.		
6 The junior clerk sometimes works at the counter.		
7 The manager is usually in his office all day.		
8 The staff leave when the bank closes.		

Finding the best word Fill in the missing words in the sentences.

1 _____ is another way of saying 'filled up again'.
2 The place where a cashier keeps his or her cash is called a _____.
3 The _____ mail is the mail which comes to the branch.
4 _____ is another way of saying 'deals with'.
5 The place where the cashiers work is called the _____.
6 The place where money can be deposited when the bank is shut is the _____.
7 The machine which gives out cash when the bank is closed is called the _____.
8 The part of the computer which is in the branch is called the 'computer _____'.

What's his job? Look at the following example:

'What's the chief clerk's job?'
'The chief clerk's job consists of *organising* the work for the day, *helping* and *advising* the staff and *taking* over from the manager when he is away.'

Using the information on the opposite page, try to describe the jobs of the following people in the same way. Do not try to include all the information.

1 A cashier.
2 The manager.
3 The senior or securities clerk.
4 The computer operator.
5 The typist/clerk.

Paragraph writing Using the notes on the opposite page, write a paragraph on what happens in the Morgantown branch of the Shoestring Bank after 3.30 in the afternoon.

16 Shoestring Bank – A Clearing Bank

As you have seen, the main functions of the Shoestring bank are as follows:

1 to accept deposits of money
2 to transfer money from these deposits to other accounts
3 to arrange for deposits to be withdrawn
4 to lend money

The Shoestring Bank is typical of real banks all over the world. For example, Barclays, Lloyds, Crédit Lyonnais, Deutsche Bank. This kind of bank is called a 'clearing bank' because of function number 2—'clearing' cheques with other banks.

The clearing system in England operates in this way:

DAY ONE		DAY TWO		DAY THREE
Shoestring Bank, The Parade, Morgantown	Shoestring Bank Clearing Dept. London	Bankers' Clearing House-Exchange Centre	Barclays Clearing Dept. London	Barclays Bank, High Street, Cambridge
1 Peter Moore pays into his account a cheque for £55 from his brother David, who banks at Barclays, High St., Cambridge.	Details of all cheques and slips are put onto microfilm.	Shoestring and Barclays exchange cheques and lists.	Receives cheques from clearing drawn on Barclays branches.	Receives David's cheque for payment.
2 The 'waste clerk' 'machines' the details of the cheque onto a list, with all the other cheques, cash and credit slips received.	Cheques from all Shoestring branches drawn on Barclays branches are put into plastic containers with the machined lists.	(There is a special department of the Clearing House called BACS, Bankers' Automated Clearing Services Limited. If a company has 'time' on a computer, it can put all its payments onto a magnetic or paper tape, which is cleared in the same way as a bundle of cheques.)	Lists are checked.	David Moore has only £36 in his account.
3 Cheques are sorted into 'bank order'—that is, put into bundles of Barclays cheques, Lloyds cheques and so on.	Vans deliver cheques and lists to the Exchange Centre at the Bankers' Clearing House.		Cheques are sorted into branch order.	Branch refuses to honour the cheque.
4 Cheques, slips and list are sent to Shoestring Clearing Dept., London, by post.			Bundles of cheques are sent by post to High Street branch, Cambridge.	Sends the cheque back directly by post to Shoestring Bank, Morgantown.

If Peter's bank *does not* hear from David's bank within 4 days, they know that Barclays have cleared the cheque and they credit Peter's account with £55.

Direct Debits: If you make payments often to one person or company but the *amount* is *not fixed* and the *timing* is *not regular*, you can give the bank an order to Direct Debit your account. This means that you give the bank permission to pay your bill direct to your creditor's bank account on demand. The person you owe money to presents his 'bill' or direct debit form to his own bank. Direct Debits and Bank Giro slips are *cleared* in the same way as cheques.

Comprehension Choose the right answer.

1 Bankers' Automated Clearing Services Ltd is a part of
  (a) Shoestring Bank (b) Shoestring Clearing Department
  (c) Barclays Clearing Department (d) Bankers' Clearing House.
2 Barclays Bank, High Street, Cambridge (a) honours the cheque (b) credits the cheque to Peter Moore (c) refuses to honour the cheque (d) clears the cheque.

Prepositions Put the correct prepositions into the spaces below.

1 If you do not have your own computer, you can buy time _____ someone else's.
2 He had only £5 _____ his account.
3 They credited his account _____ £124.
4 Depending on the banks they came from, the cheques are sorted _____ branch order.
5 My sister banks _____ Lloyds in Birmingham.
6 They refused to honour the cheque _____ £26 that you gave me.
7 Have you paid that cheque I gave you _____ your account yet?
8 This cheque has Barclays, Westminster Road, Heaton on it. It must be drawn _____ that branch.
9 If the cheque is not accepted, you will hear from us _____ 4 days.

Talking about how systems work 2

In Unit 14 we looked at one way of describing a system. Sometimes we want to show that things happened in a time sequence. For example:

Peter received a cheque from his brother. He paid it into his bank.
'After (Peter) receiving a cheque from his brother, Peter paid it into his bank.'
OR
The cheques are put into plastic containers with the machined lists. They are delivered by van to the Bankers' Clearing House.
'Before (the cheques) being delivered by van to the Bankers' Clearing House, the cheques are put into plastic containers with the machined lists.'

Note: We do not say the words in brackets, but we 'understand' that they are there. They must be the same as the subject of the second part of the sentence.

Using the information below, make sentences with *before -ing* and *after -ing*.

1 David's bank refused to honour the cheque. They sent it back to Peter's bank.
2 The 'waste clerk' receives the details of all the cheques and credit slips. She machines them onto a list.
3 The clearing department puts all the details onto microfilm. They send the cheques to the Bankers' Clearing House.
4 You must sign your travellers cheques. You leave the bank. (Unit 13)
5 The bank converts your travellers cheques into local currency. They take an exchange commission for the transaction. (Unit 13)
6 The staff sometimes meet to discuss problems. They leave the bank. (Unit 15)

17 The Bank of England

The Bank of England plays a very important part in international finance. It does business with many international institutions and the central banks of many countries keep their accounts there. It advises banks, companies and even governments.

In England, however, the Bank has three main functions:

1 Banker to the Government

The Bank of England gives the government the same service that any bank gives to its customers, including advice on financial matters. In addition to this, it has the following functions:
a) It holds the central accounts of the Government – the accounts of H M Exchequer and of the National Loans Fund. Any money received or paid out by the central government goes through these accounts.
b) It arranges short-term borrowing of money for the government.
c) It manages the government's stocks. There are nearly 200 types of stock with a nominal value of £20,000,000,000! The Bank issues the stocks, keeps a list of the three million stockholders and pays out the dividends when they are ready – a total of 6 million payments a year. This is the area where most people are employed.
d) It manages the Exchange Equalisation Account. This means making sure the exchange value of sterling does not change too much (see Unit 11). It controls the country's reserves of gold and foreign currencies and administers the Exchange Control Regulations. This is an important job because sterling is an international currency.

In short, it is the central bank of the United Kingdom.

2 The 'Bankers' Bank'

The principal banks in England are the 'high street' banks, e.g. Lloyds, Barclays, Midland. They all keep a large amount of their cash in the Bank of England. In fact, it acts as the principal bank for all the other banks. It also has close relations with the major British banking organisations, such as the Committee of London Clearing Banks and the British Banker's Association, as well as with the Stock Exchange and the insurance industry.

It really is the bank of bankers.

3 The issuer of bank notes

If you look at any English bank note, you will see:

BANK OF ENGLAND
I promise to pay the bearer on demand the sum of £___

For the Governor and Company of the Bank of England

(signature)
Chief Cashier.

In the beginning, any bank could issue these 'promises to pay' but the Bank Act of 1844 changed that. Now, only the Bank of England can issue notes. Until 1931 it was possible to take a bank note to the Bank of England and exchange it for the same amount of gold. Nowadays, the value of a bank note does not depend on gold, but on a complicated system of government securities. The 'promise to pay' in gold or other money has become money itself.

True or false? Look at the sentences below and tick (√) if you think they are true or false. Can you correct the false statements?

	TRUE	FALSE

1. The Bank of England only does business in England.
2. The British government banks with the Bank of England.
3. The total nominal value of the government's stocks is two thousand million pounds.
4. Any bank in England can issue bank notes.
5. The Bank of England can help to control the exchange rate of sterling.
6. The Bank of England deals only with the government and other banks.

Finding the best word Fill in the missing words in the sentences. The words in brackets () have a similar meaning to the missing words.

1. Managing the government's stocks is one of the Bank's f........ (jobs)
2. The n...... value of a £100 stock certificate is £100. (face value)
3. If you invest your money in stocks, your profit comes in regular payments called d.........
4. The supplies of gold and foreign currencies that a country has are called its r........
5. Barclays and Lloyds are p........ banks
6. The m.... banking organisations are the biggest ones.

What does *it* mean? Look at this sentence from the opposite page:

'It advises banks, companies and even governments.'

What does *it* mean? If we look at the sentences before this one in the text, we find that *it* means the Bank of England. We use words like *it*, *they* and *there* so that we do not have to repeat words that we have to use often.

Look at the following sentences and say what the words in italics mean. Some of the sentences are from other units.

1. The central banks of many countries keep their accounts *there*.
2. *This* is the area where most staff are employed.
3. *They* all keep large amounts of their cash in the Bank of England.
4. *It* really is the bank of bankers.
5. Who shall I make *it* payable to? (Unit 5)
6. So an adult can have *both* then? (Unit 9)
7. Would you prefer *them* in pounds sterling or in dollars? (Unit 12)
8. I find the easiest way of getting money *here* is with an open credit arrangement. (Unit 13)

Answering questions Write complete questions using the following notes. Can you answer the questions?

1. Which bank/central bank/United Kingdom?
2. Where/High Street banks keep/large amount/cash?
3. Where/you see/words 'Bank of England – I promise to pay ...'?
4. In/beginning, who/issue/promises to pay?
5. Nowadays, what/value/bank note depend on?

18 The changing face of banking

The Seventeenth century

In the middle of the 17th century, people used to leave their money and gold with goldsmiths. These men made jewellery (rings, chains, etc.) out of gold. Because they had to keep a lot of gold in their shops, they used to have very safe places to keep it. When people deposited money, the goldsmiths used to give them a receipt. After a while, people used to exchange their notes instead of the money and gold which they represented. The goldsmiths also used to lend money both to individuals and to the government.

The Twentieth century

In England and Wales today, there are four major clearing banks: Barclays, Lloyds, the Midland and the National Westminster. These banks, known as the Big Four, and 3 smaller ones do most of the day-to-day banking. In fact, they do the same job as the goldsmiths used to do 300 years ago. This work is done by over 200,000 staff in over 12,000 branches.

In the last 20 years, banks have become industries in strong competition with each other and other financial institutions.

The future

The face of banking is changing rapidly. Modern technology has given banks:

a) **automatic cash points** — where customers can draw out cash and get a current balance, even when the bank is closed.

b) **electronic calculators** — to calculate, for example, foreign exchange rates very quickly.

c) **electronic coin-counters** — which count coins much faster than a cashier can.

AND COMPUTERS

Perhaps the most important development is the introduction of computers. These wonderful machines do a lot of the routine work of the bank — but much faster than people can.

Computers can:

1 KEEP RECORDS — not only of customers' accounts but also of personal information. This information can be shown as a display on a video screen or printed out on paper. There are even computers that can give a spoken answer to a spoken question.

2 SORT CHEQUES — It is possible now by using special systems to sort cheques completely by computer. The computer reads the bank sort code and other information written in magnetic ink at the bottom of the cheque.

3 CHECK SIGNATURES — when you open an account you give the bank a copy of your signature — a specimen — which is stored in the computer. The clerk can check any signature against a visual display of this specimen on the computer.

Computers play a part in much of the daily banking business you have studied in this book. Credit transfer and direct debiting are only two examples. Most bankers agree that the time saved by computers should be spent on improving personal services for their customers.

Comprehension Choose the best answer.

1 People used to leave money with goldsmiths because (a) they made jewellery (b) they kept gold in their shops (c) they had safe places to keep it (d) they lent money.
2 How many small clearing banks are there in England? (a) 300 (b) 3 (c) 4 (d) 7.

Word puzzle

You can find words hidden horizontally or vertically in this puzzle. Use the clues to help you. The first word is marked for you.

Clues

1 A short letter (n . . .)
2 A paper saying you have received something (r . . . . . .)
3 Information which is kept (r . . . . . .)
4 Rings, earrings, bracelets (j . . . .)
5 The number of major clearing banks in England and Wales (f . . .)
6 To have the same opinion (a . . . .)
7 The part of the video where the picture appears (s . . . . .)
8 The words and figures that appear on a video (d . . . . . .)
9 A hundred years (c . . . . . .)
10 Regular, normal, everyday (r . . . . . .)

R	O	L	M	P	L	T	S	U	J
E	R	E	C	E	I	P	T	P	E
C	O	V	A	R	E	R	E	O	W
O	U	L	S	C	R	E	E	N	E
R	T	E	H	O	E	S	P	O	L
D	I	S	P	L	A	Y	A	T	L
S	N	S	O	L	A	G	R	E	E
O	E	N	Z	P	T	F	O	U	R
C	C	E	N	T	U	R	Y	R	Y
H	O	R	S	L	E	P	A	Y	E

Things which no longer happen

'In the middle of the seventeenth century, people *used to* leave their money and gold with the goldsmiths.'

When we have an action which a) happened regularly in the past and b) does not happen now, we can use the expression *used to* + *infinitive* instead of the simple past tense.

Fill in the gaps with *used to* and an infinitive, using the information on the opposite page. Then write the sentences in full.

1 Because goldsmiths kept/lot of gold/shops/ . . . . very safe places/keep it.
2 When people gave money/goldsmiths/they . . . . them/ note/receipt.
3 Later, people . . . . notes/instead/money/gold.
4 Both individuals/government . . . . money/from/ goldsmiths.
5 Clearing banks/same job today/goldsmiths . . . . years ago.

Modern banking

By answering the questions, write a paragraph about computers in banking. Begin your sentences with the words in brackets.

1 What is the most important development as far as modern banking is concerned? (The most . . . .)
2 What can computers keep records of as well as customers' accounts? (Computers can . . . .)
3 How does a computer sort all the cheques? (A computer . . . .)
4 How can signatures be checked? (Signatures . . . .)
5 How should time saved by computers be spent? (Time . . . .)

Answers

(/ means there are alternative answers)

1 Why have a bank account?

Comprehension
1 (d) 2 (a), (d)

Hidden word puzzle
1 cash 2 security 3 advice 4 loan
5 amount 6 advantage 7 shortage
Hidden word: ACCOUNT

Where to find information in this book
1 Unit 8 2 Units 3, 4, 5 and 6 3 Units 11, 12 and 13 4 Units 8 and 9 5 Units 8 and 10 6 Unit 9

Helping a friend (sample answers)
1 You can pay by cheque.
2 If you put your money into a deposit account, it will earn interest for you.
3 You can get travellers cheques and order foreign currency from a bank. In many European countries, shops and banks accept your normal cheques as Eurocheques.
4 A bank can advise you on money problems in general. It can help you by lending you money and also with things like buying a house and running a business.

2 Opening an account?

True or false?
1 False. You have to put in a minimum of £1.
2 True.
3 False. Two people can have a joint account.
4 True.

Hidden word puzzle
1 salary 2 free 3 counterfoil
4 open 5 branch 6 specimen
7 coins 8 clerk 9 notes
Hidden word: REFERENCE

Giving instructions (sample answers)
1 You should put it in the place where it says 'Account Number'.
2 Write the amount in the place where it says 'Notes'.
3 Put the amount/it in the place where it says 'Coins: 50p'.
4 Fill it/the address in, in the place where it says 'Account holding branch'. OR Fill in the address in the place where it says 'Account holding branch'.
5 Could you put it/your signature in the place where it says 'Paid in by'?
6 Fill in the total in the place where it says 'Total of cash'. OR Fill it/the total in, in the place where it says 'Total of cash'.

Writing questions (sample answers)
1 Q: What do you give to the bank when you open a bank account?
   A: The names and addresses of two people and a specimen signature.
2 Q: How much do you need to open a bank account in England?
   A: £1.
3 Q: What is an example of your signature called?
   A: A specimen signature.
4 Q: What do you (have to) pay the bank for its services?
   A: A commission or account charge.
5 Q: How can you get these services free of charge?
   A: If you keep a certain amount of credit in your account/By keeping a certain amount of credit in your account.

3 How to use a cheque book

Comprehension
1 (c) 2 (d)

Finding the best word
1 withdraw 2 balance
3 counterfoil 4 valid 5 in ink

Numbers
2 £170.37 A hundred and seventy pounds, thirty-seven pence/p.
3 £26.60 Twenty-six pounds, sixty pence/p.
4 £875.28 Eight hundred and seventy-five pounds, twenty-eight pence/p.
5 £926.61 Nine hundred and twenty-six pounds, sixty-one pence/p.
6 £1,144.60 One thousand, one hundred and forty-four pounds, sixty pence/p.

Guided summary: Using a cheque book
(sample answers)
1 Each cheque is printed with the account holder's name and the account number.
2 The cheque is only valid when it is signed and dated.
3 If you want to take money out of the bank to spend, you write 'CASH' or 'SELF' after the word 'Pay'.
4 The amount should be written in ink in words and figures and as far to the left as possible.
5 You can keep a record of how much you have spent on the stub or counterfoil.
6 The bank has an obligation to honour the cheque if you have this much money in your account.

4 Security

True or false?
1 False. Vaults are special rooms where cash is kept.
2 False. You can only sign a cheque which has your own name on it.
3 True.
4 False. A crossed cheque must pass through the payee's bank account.
5 False. A standing order is used for regular fixed payments.

Hidden word puzzle
1 cash 2 open 3 complex
4 counter 5 order 6 fixed 7 steal
8 payee
Hidden word: SECURITY

The pickpocket's dream
1 – Fill in today's date.
 – Put his own name as payee.
 – Write any amount he likes in words and figures in the spaces Mary has left at the beginning of the line. (It could be nine hundred!)
 – Take the cheque along to a bank and ask them to cash it over the counter. (The cheque is not crossed so the pickpocket does not have to have a bank account in order to receive the money.)

2 (Sample answers)
You should write the amount in words and figures as near to the left as possible.

You should use crossed cheques so that it is more difficult for a thief to cash them.

You should fill in the name of the payee before you sign the cheque.

You should throw away any cheque which you have started to write and then decided not to use.

You should not sign a cheque before you have filled in all the other details.

You should not leave any room for another person to write extra words or figures.

Filling in a Bank Giro slip

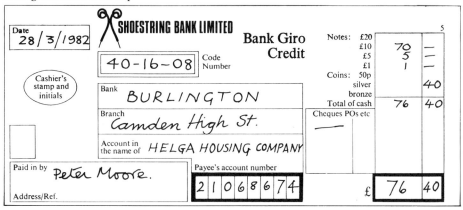

5 Your current account in operation

Comprehension
1 (d) 2 (c)

Finding the best word
1 payable 2 dispenser 3 readout
4 slot 5 Tap 6 proceed 7 cancel

Instructions
If you need cash, press 'withdrawal'.
If you press 'proceed' the viewer shows you what you have asked for.
If you ask for cash, the machine checks with a central computer.
If you put your cash card in the slot, this will open the machine.
If you need a statement of your balance, press 'enquiry'.
If you press 'enquiry', you will see your balance in the viewer.

Guided paragraph writing
Yesterday, Mrs Dobbs went to Miami Fashions to buy a dress. It costs £41.20. She paid by cheque and cheque card and made the cheque out to/payable to Miami Fashions Limited. By mistake, she wrote £31.20 and she had to correct it and initial the correction. The assistant was very helpful.

6 In the red

True or false?
1 True.
2 False. They have an agreed limit of £120.
3 True. £152.54 to be exact.
4 False. The bank has had to honour the cheque because it was written with a cheque card.

Finding the word
The statement

1 overdrawn 2 statement 3 in credit 4 in the red 5 credit
6 account charge

The letter

1 enclose 2 agreed limit 3 Yours sincerely 4 Dear

Being polite
1 Could you (just) . . . . ?
2 There you are./Here you are. Here's your dress.
3 Could you tell me . . . . ?
4 Just a moment.
5 Certainly.

Dialogue: At the bank
(specimen dialogue) (answers only)
Could you tell me the balance of my account please?
Certainly. It's . . . . . .
Just a moment, I've given you my cheque card number. My account number is 0275936.
Here you are/There you are/Here's your balance.

7 Credit cards

Reading comprehension

ACCORD	SHOESTRINGER	FLEXICARD
YES	YES	YES
—	YES	—
YES-min £100	—	£200
£100	—	£50
—	YES	—
2 months	1 month	1 month
—	YES	—
YES	—	YES
—	£25	—
10%	—	5%

Finding the best word

1 personal   2 advance   3 monthly
4 additional   5 abroad   6 charge
7 unauthorized   8 maximum
9 liability   10 nationwide

Using a credit card

Conversation 1
a) He is talking on the telephone to someone in a theatre box office.
b) He wants 2 balcony seats for Thursday 31st.

Conversation 2
a) She is in the office of a car hire firm.
b) She is hiring a car.
c) Can I pay by Flexicard?

Conversation 3
a) He is at an airline desk at an airport.
b) He is paying for a plane ticket.
c) Do you take Shoestringer?

8 Borrowing money

True or false?

1 False. The bank only asks you for security if it thinks you are a bad risk.
2 True.
3 False. The rate of interest on a personal loan is fixed.
4 True.
5 False. It depends on your income and monthly expenses.

Finding the best word

1 daily   2 fixed   3 notice
4 expensive   5 security   6 repayments

Numbers

*1 If you borrow three hundred pounds and pay it back over eighteen months, the total amount payable is three hundred and forty-eight pounds seventy-three p, the interest is forty-eight pounds seventy-three p and you make eighteen monthly repayments of nineteen pounds thirty-seven p.

*2 If you borrow two thousand, three hundred and fifty pounds and pay it back over thirty months, the total amount payable is two thousand nine hundred and ninety pounds forty p, the interest is six hundred and forty pounds forty p and you make thirty monthly repayments of ninety-nine pounds sixty-eight p.

*3 If you borrow three thousand pounds and pay it back over thirty-six months, the total amount payable is three thousand, nine hundred and eighty-nine pounds, eighty-two p, the interest is nine hundred and eighty-nine pounds, eighty-two p and you make thirty-six repayments of a hundred and ten pounds eighty-two p.

Guided writing

1 If I needed 18 months for repayment, I would ask for a personal loan.
2 If I had no security, I would ask for an overdraft.
3 If I wanted a fixed interest rate, I would ask for a personal loan.
4 If I needed a little extra money sometimes, I would ask for an overdraft.
5 If I wanted to borrow £2,000, I would ask for a personal loan.

9 Deposit accounts and investment

True or false?

1 False. A deposit account is for saving money whereas a current account is for day-to-day finances.
2 True.
3 False. You can also use a Giro credit slip.
4 True.

Using the right expression

1 (c) 2 (d) 3 (c) 4 (d)

Comparing alternatives
(sample answers)

1 .... whereas both adults and children can use deposit accounts.
2 .... whereas it does in a deposit account.
3 .... whereas you use withdrawal slips to take money out of a deposit account.
4 .... whereas with a deposit account you should give a week's notice.

Asking questions (sample answers)

1 Q: Which form should/do/must I use to withdraw money from a deposit account?
  A: A withdrawal slip/form.
2 Q: Which form should/do/must I use to pay money in?
  A: One of the forms from your paying-in book or a credit slip.
3 Q: How much notice should/do I give before I withdraw money?
  A: You should give a week's notice. You can give less than this but you will lose some interest if you do.
4 Q: How can/do I move money from my current account to a/my deposit account?
  A: { By / With a } Standing order.
5 Q: What is a good form of investment for the short-term saver?
  A: A deposit account.
6 Q: What rate of interest do you get with a Special Savings Account?
  A: 1% above the normal rate.

Note on Question 6:
'You' can be used to mean 'one' or 'a person'.
Questions 1–5 could be asked in this way, too.

10 Running a business

Comprehension

1 (c) 2 (d) 3 (a)

Hidden word puzzle

1 plan 2 purchase 3 loan
4 figures 5 advise 6 up-to-date
7 private 8 variable 9 monthly
10 term
Hidden word: PROFITABLE

Being formal

1 Thank you very much.
2 I enclose ......
3 I should perhaps explain ......
4 Might I suggest that we ......
5 Perhaps you would be kind enough to telephone ......
6 I would be most grateful if you would ......
7 Please do not hesitate to contact me ......

Letter writing (sample answer)

> Adams Flower Shop,
> 69 High Street,
> Morgantown.
> 29 December, 1982
>
> Your Ref: JW/GB
> J Walker Esq.,
> Manager,
> Shoestring Bank Limited,
> 7 The Parade,
> Morgantown.
>
> Dear Mr Walker,
>
> Thank you very much for your letter of 22 December. I enclose the information which you requested.
>
> Thank you for your offer of a meeting. I am extremely sorry for not telephoning. I have been away for Christmas. I am coming into the bank next Monday. Might I suggest that we arrange a time then? If you are not free, perhaps you would be kind enough to give your secretary a list of suitable times.
>
> I look forward to seeing you. Thank you very much for your help.
>
> Yours sincerely,
>
> *E. L. Adams*
>
> E L Adams

11 Foreign exchange

True or false?

1 True.
2 False. A bank usually charges a commission for cashing a travellers cheque. In the list in this unit it costs £1 per person.
3 False. The price of a currency can change dramatically depending on the economic and political situation in the country and the exchange controls fixed by the government of that country.
4 A bank always wants to give away as little as possible on a deal. If we take the example given of the exchange buying and selling rates for US dollars, the two rates are 2.2915 and 2.2925.
If an English bank is selling dollars, it wants to give as few as possible for each pound it receives. So it gives the lowest number, which is 2.2915.
If an American tourist comes into the bank with dollars to sell, wanting to buy English currency, the English bank wants to get as many dollars as possible for each pound it sells, so it gives the higher number, which is 2.2925. So the bank always SELLS LOW – BUYS HIGH.

Word puzzle

2 escudos   3 commission   4 Holland
5 USA   6 Denmark   7 control
8 drachma   9 Yugoslavia   10 dealer
11 quoted/fixed

Calculating exchange rates

1 They would cost him 359 Austrian schillings. That is 35.9×10.
2 £42.84. That is $£\dfrac{1}{2.28} \times \$100 = £43.84$
less £1 commission.
3 Swiss francs 450.74. That is £100 less 50p commission = £99.50p.
£99.50 × 4.53 Swiss francs to the pound = 450.74 Swiss francs.
4 £48.32. That is: each person has
1700 Belgian francs. $\dfrac{1700}{84.5} = £20$
each person has 28 guilders $\dfrac{28}{5.64} = £4.964$
total = £24.96
less 40p commission for each currency = £24.16
together they have £48.32.

The bank charges each person commission. If they had put their money together and one person had changed it all, they could have saved the 80p commission which the second person also paid.

Guided summary:
Foreign exchange rates

Dealers from over 200 banks round the world fix foreign exchange rates. These rates change every day. The 'price' of a country's currency often depends on the economic and political situation, amongst other things. The Foreign Exchange always quotes two prices for each currency – a selling price and a buying price. Banks always sell low and buy high.

12 Ordering travellers cheques and foreign currency

Comprehension

TRAVELLERS CHEQUES AND FOREIGN CURRENCY ORDER FORM

Please supply travellers cheques and currency as shown below for collection on `19 June` 19___ Please allow at least three working days before collection date.

TRAVELLERS CHEQUES

QUANTITY	VALUE	QUANTITY	VALUE
	at £10		at $20
	at £20	10	at $50 $500
	at £50		at $100
	at £100		at $500
Total Value £		Total Value $ 500	

TICK BOX

FOREIGN CURRENCY

	£		£
Austria	£	Portugal	£
Belgium	£20	Spain	£
France	£	Sweden	£20
Greece	£	Switzerland	£
Holland	£20	USA	£
Italy	£	W. Germany	£20
Norway	£20	Yugoslavia	£
		Other	£

I will pay by Shoestringer ☐
I will pay cash ☐
Please debit my account no. **02468391** Name **D. L. WATSON**
Address
Daytime telephone number **01-496-4083**
Signature
Date **16 June**

Choosing the right word
1 (d) 2 (c) 3 (a) 4 (c) 5 (c)

Changing reported speech into direct speech

Questions
1 Can I help you?
2 Do you have an account at this branch?
3 And you'd like some currency?
4 Shall I debit your account?
5 When would you like them?

Statements
1 I'd like to order some foreign currency please.
2 My name's Watson.
3 I'll deal with the travellers cheques first.
4 I'll take ten 50s please.
5 I'm leaving on 20th June.

Dialogue writing (sample answer)

MARY: I'd like to order some foreign currency and travellers cheques please.
CLERK: Do you have an account at this branch please?
MARY: Yes. My account number is 04968288.
CLERK: I'll deal with the travellers cheques first. Would you prefer them in pounds sterling or dollars?
MARY: Pounds please.
CLERK: They come in £10, £20, £50 and £100 denominations.
MARY: I'll take five 20s and four 50s please.
CLERK: And you'd like some currency?
MARY: Yes, I'm going to Spain and Portugal so I'd better take £15 worth of each of Spanish pesetas and Portuguese escudos.
CLERK: Well, that's £30 worth of currency and £300 in travellers cheques. Shall I debit your account?
MARY: No I'd like to pay by Shoestringer please?
CLERK: Fine. And when would you like them?
MARY: In four days' time on 24 March please.
CLERK: Right. Could I have your telephone number and I'll call you when they're ready.
MARY: Yes. It's Morgantown 28631.
CLERK: Thank you. Goodbye.
MARY: Goodbye.

13 What do you do if you need money in other countries?

True or false?
1. False. You give your bank at home a copy of your signature and they send it to the foreign bank.
2. False. You can only withdraw money up to a limit that you have already agreed with the bank.
3. False. Open credit is best for people who are staying in one place for some time. Travellers cheques and Eurocheques (in Europe) are more useful for people who are travelling from country to country.
4. False. They are the same cheques that are issued by banks in European countries.
5. False. In some countries they can be used to pay for goods and services too.
6. True.
7. True.
8. False. If you telex your bank at home, they can usually give you some replacement cheques or cash in a short time.

Hidden word puzzle
1 charge 2 calculates 3 agreed
4 converted 5 serial 6 stolen
7 countersign 8 safe 9 replacement
Hidden word: GUARANTEE

Using your travellers cheques (sample answers)
1. On 20 June, he cashed a $20 cheque, serial number 026489 at the Skandinaviska Enskilda Banken.
2. On 22 June, he paid his bill at the Hotel Kramer, in Malmö with a $50 cheque, serial number 069801 and a $20 cheque, serial number 026490.
3. On 23 June he cashed a $100 cheque, serial number 096942 at the Deutsche Bank in Hamburg.
4. On 26 June, he paid his bill at the Hotel Atlantic, Hamburg with a $100 cheque, serial number 096943.
5. On the same day he paid for his airline ticket to Brussels, with a $100 cheque, serial number 096944.
6. On the following day, 27 June, he bought a present for his wife at the Bloch Department store in Brussels and paid for it with a $20 cheque, serial number 026491.
7. On the same day, he cashed two cheques at the Banque Nationale in Brussels: a $20 cheque, serial number 026492 and a $50 cheque, serial number 069802.
8. On the following day, June 28 he bought a ferry ticket from the Hook of Holland back to England and paid for it with his last travellers cheque, a $20 cheque, serial number 026493.

Writing a dialogue
(sample answer)
CLERK: Can I help you?
MARY: Yes. I'd like to cash these cheques for $120 please.
CLERK: Could you countersign and date them all please?
MARY: Here you are.
CLERK: Thank you. Could I have your passport please?
MARY: Yes, certainly. Here you are.
CLERK: Thank you. Just a moment please.
....
CLERK: That's ten thousand four hundred and forty pesetas, less a hundred pesetas encashment charge. Here's your receipt.
MARY: Thank you very much. Goodbye.
CLERK: Goodbye.

14 Sending money abroad

Comprehension
1. By Telegraphic (Cable) Transfer.
2. By International Money Order.
3. No. Only in £ sterling or US dollars.
4. By International Money Transfer.
5. By International Money Order or Foreign Draft.

Choosing the right word
1 (d) 2 (b) 3 (c) 4 (d)

Talking about how systems work
is debited, are filled in, is transferred, is sent, is converted, is withdrawn, is credited, is informed, is collected.

Guided writing: Writing questions
(sample answers)
1. How long does it take to send a Telegraphic or Cable Transfer?/How long does a Telegraphic or Cable Transfer take?
2. Who sends the money when you pay by Foreign Draft/Cable Transfer/International Money Order?
3. Must an International Money Order/ International Money Transfer go through a bank account?
4. What charges are there with an International Money Order?/Who pays the charges for an International Money Order?
5. How is a Telegraphic or Cable Transfer sent?

15 A day in the life of the bank

True or false?

1 False. The staff in a small branch have to be able to do many different jobs.
2 False. Two members of staff arrive early to open the bank.
3 True.
4 False. The manager and chief clerk open the safe.
5 True.
6 True.
7 False. The manager often visits customers' offices and businesses.
8 False. The staff leave about an hour after the bank closes.

Finding the best word

1 refilled   2 till   3 incoming
4 handles   5 counter   6 night safe
7 cash dispenser   8 terminal

What's his job?

1 A cashier's job consists of working at the counter, and taking in and paying out money.
2 The manager's job consists of replying to his letters, having interviews and visiting his customers.
3 The senior clerk's job consists of handling the difficult paperwork and the problems which need expert knowledge.
4 The computer operator's job consists of entering all the customers' credits and debits through the computer terminal.
5 The typist/clerk's job consists of dealing with the mail, handling enquiries and being responsible for standing orders.

Guided paragraph writing

At 3.30 the bank closes. The chief clerk organises the work for the rest of the staff and the typist organises the outgoing mail. The cashiers and the junior clerk clear their desks and balance their cash. They return the cash from their tills to the safe. The staff finish the 'business of the day'. They sometimes meet to discuss important problems or other matters. They leave between 4.30 and 5.00.

16 Shoestring Bank – a clearing bank

Comprehension

1 (d)   2 (c)

Prepositions

1 on   2 in   3 with   4 into   5 at (with)
6 for   7 into   8 on   9 within/in

Talking about how systems work 2

1 After refusing to honour David's cheque, his bank sent it back to Peter's bank.
2 After receiving the details of all the cheques and credit slips, the waste clerk machines them onto a list.
3 Before sending the cheques to the Bankers' Clearing House, the clearing department puts all the details onto microfilm.
   OR   After putting all the details onto microfilm, the clearing department sends the cheques to the Bankers' Clearing House.
4 Before leaving the bank, you must sign your travellers cheques.
5 After converting your travellers cheques into local currency, the bank take an exchange commission for the transaction.
   OR   Before taking an exchange commission for the transaction, the bank converts your travellers cheques into local currency.
6 Before leaving the bank, the staff sometimes meet to discuss problems.
   OR   After sometimes meeting to discuss problems, the staff leave the bank.

17 The Bank of England

True or false?
1 False. The Bank of England does business with many international organisations.
2 True.
3 False. The total nominal value of the government's stocks is twenty thousand million pounds.
4 False. Only the Bank of England can issue bank notes in England.
5 True.
6 False. The Bank of England deals with many other financial institutions too.

Finding the best word
1 functions   2 nominal   3 dividends
4 reserves   5 principal   6 major

What does it mean?
1 at the Bank of England   2 managing government stocks   3 the principal banks   4 the Bank of England   5 my cheque   6 a deposit account and a current account   7 the travellers cheques   8 to Bahrain

Answering questions (sample answers)
1 Which bank is the central bank of the United Kingdom? The Bank of England.
2 Where do the High Street banks keep a large amount of their cash? In the Bank of England./They keep it in the Bank of England.
3 Where will/can/do you see the words – 'Bank of England – I promise to pay . . .'? On any English bank note./If you look at any English bank note.
4 In the beginning, who could issue these promises to pay? Any bank. Any bank could issue them.
5 Nowadays, what does the value of a bank note depend on? It depends on a complicated system of government securities.

18 The changing face of banking

Comprehension
1 (c)   2 (b)

Word puzzle
1 note   2 receipt   3 records
4 jewellery   5 four   6 agree
7 screen   8 display   9 century
10 routine

Things which no longer happen
1 Because the goldsmiths kept a lot of gold in their shops, they used to have very safe places to keep it.
2 When people gave money to the goldsmiths, they used to give them a note or receipt.
3 Later, people used to exchange notes instead of money and gold.
4 Both individuals and the government used to borrow money from the goldsmiths.
5 The clearing banks do the same job today as the goldsmiths used to do years ago.

Modern banking (sample answer)
The most important development as far as modern banking is concerned is the introduction of computers. Computers can keep records of personal information as well as of customers' accounts. A computer sorts all the cheques by reading the bank sort code and other information written in magnetic ink at the bottom of the cheques. Signatures can be checked against a visual display of a specimen signature on the computer. Time which is saved by computers should be spent on improving personal services for customers.

LONGMAN GROUP LIMITED
*Longman House, Burnt Mill, Harlow,
Essex CM20 2JE, England
and Associated Companies throughout the World.*

© Longman Group Limited 1982
All rights reserved. No part of this publication may be reproduced, stored in a retrieval system, or transmitted in any form or by any means, electronic, mechanical, photocopying, recording, or otherwise, without the prior permission of the Copyright owner.

First published 1982
Second impression 1983
ISBN 0 582 74858 5

Set in Monotype Apollo
Printed in Hong Kong by
Commonwealth Printing Press Ltd.

Acknowledgements

We are grateful to the following for permission to reproduce copyright photographs:

Bank of England for page 35; Dresdner Bank for page 27; Lloyds Bank Limited for page 11.

Illustrators: Graham Allen, pages 1, 9 and 37.
Tony Morris, pages 11, 17, 19 and 27.

Cover illustration by Steve Pickard.

Filmset by Reproduction Drawings Ltd., Sutton, Surrey.